TOP▶REQUESTED
C[OUNTRY] [SHEET] [MUSIC]

13 POPULAR HITS ARRANGED BY DAN COATES

Contents

Produced by
Alfred Music
P.O. Box 10003
Van Nuys, CA 91410-0003
alfred.com

Printed in USA.

ISBN-10: 1-4706-1047-7
ISBN-13: 978-1-4706-1047-0
Cover photo: Maroon wood background: © Shutterstock / s_oleg
American West rodeo cowboy traditional: © Shutterstock / Olivier Le Queinec

Alfred Cares. Contents printed on 100% recycled paper.

AMAZED

Words and Music by Marv Green,
Aimee Mayo, and Chris Lindsey
Arranged by Dan Coates

I can hear your thoughts, I can see your— dreams.

Chorus:

I don't know how you do what you do.— I'm so in love with you. It just keeps get-ting bet-

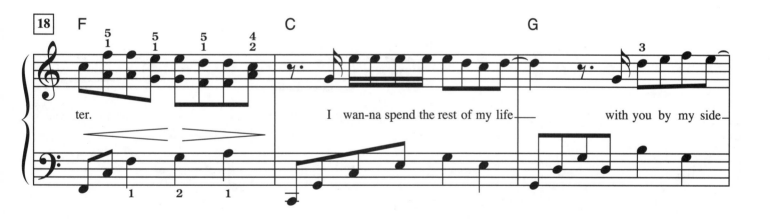

ter. I wan-na spend the rest of my life— with you by my side—

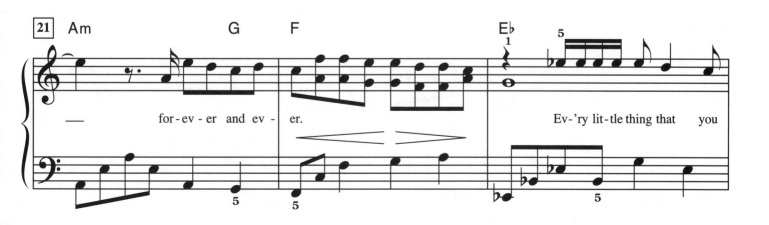

— for-ev-er and ev-er. Ev-'ry lit-tle thing that you

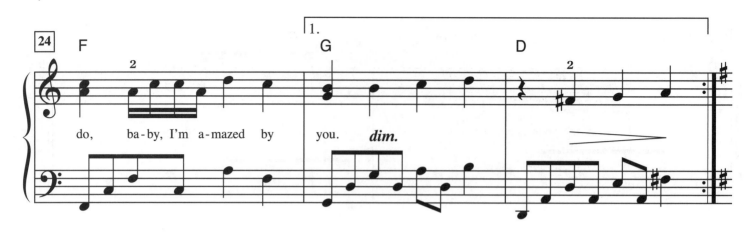

do, ba-by, I'm a-mazed by you. *dim.*

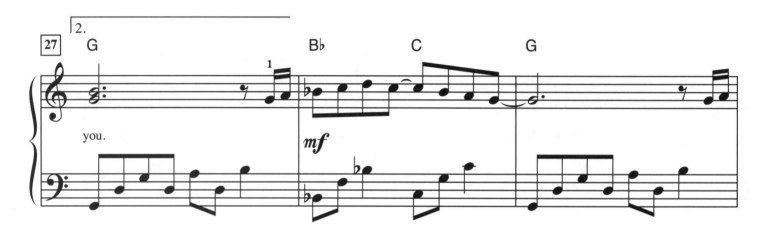

you. *mf*

f Ev-'ry lit-tle thing that you do,— I'm so in love with

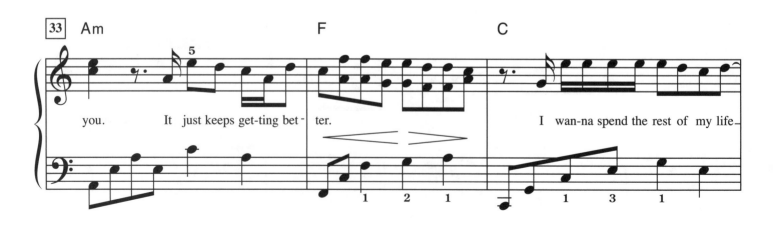

you. It just keeps get-ting bet- ter. I wan-na spend the rest of my life—

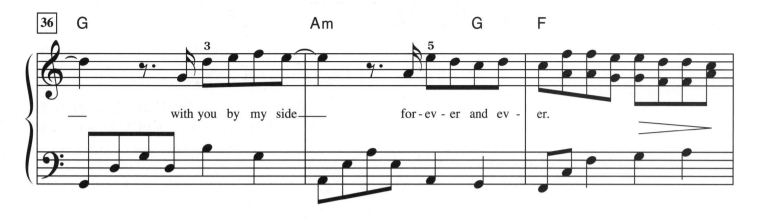

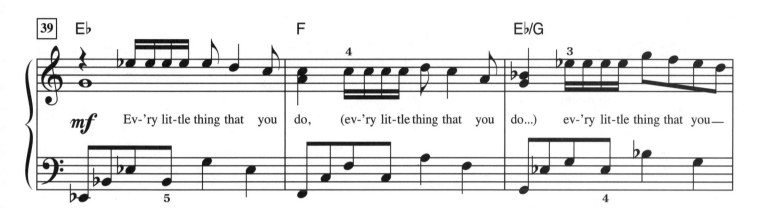

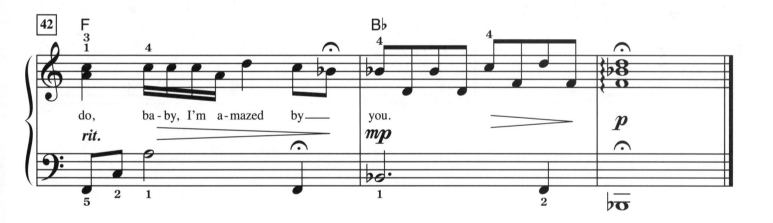

Verse 2:
The smell of your skin,
The taste of your kiss,
The way you whisper in the dark.
Your hair all around me,
Baby, you surround me.
You touch every place in my heart.
Oh, it feels like the first time every time.
I wanna spend the whole night in your eyes.
(To Chorus:)

ALL-AMERICAN GIRL

Words and Music by Carrie Underwood,
Kelley Lovelace and Ashley Gorley
Arranged by Dan Coates

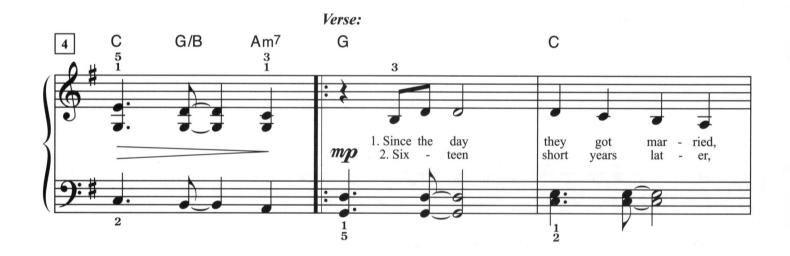

Verse:

1. Since the day   they got   mar - ried,
2. Six - teen   short years   lat - er,

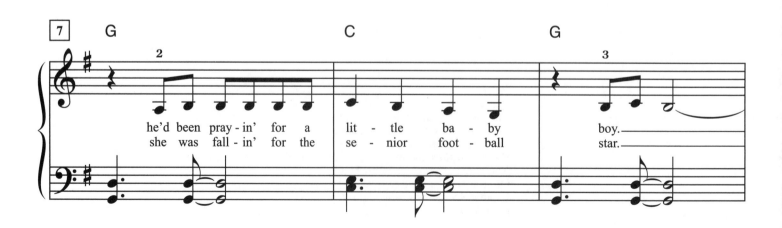

he'd been pray - in' for a   lit - tle ba - by   boy.____
she was fall - in' for the   se - nior foot - ball   star.____

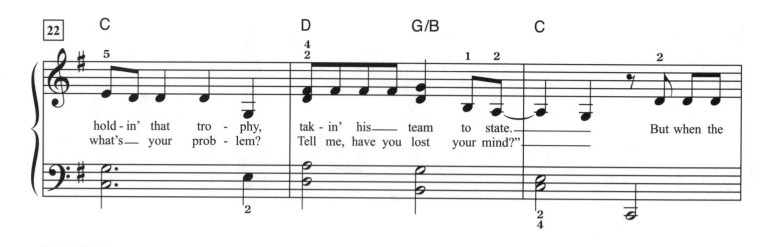

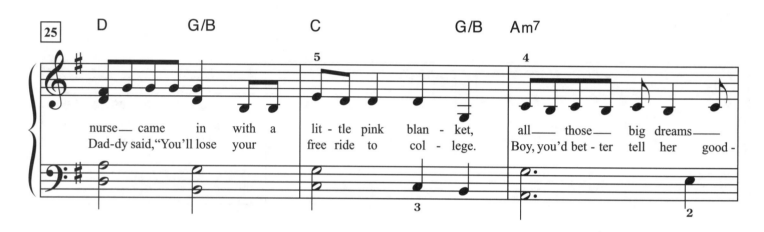

Chorus:

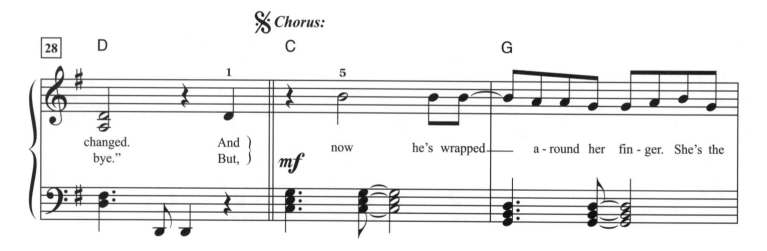

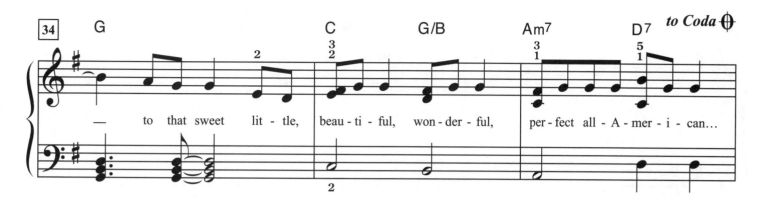

to Coda

to that sweet lit-tle, beau-ti-ful, won-der-ful, per-fect all-A-mer-i-can...

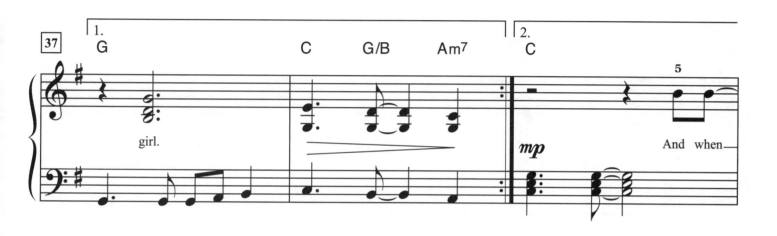

girl. And when

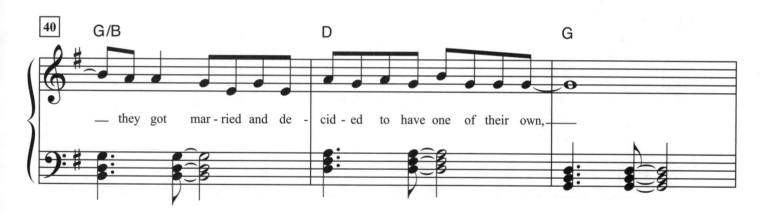

— they got mar-ried and de-cid-ed to have one of their own,—

she said, "Be hon-est, tell me what you want." And he said, "Hon-ey, you ought-a know,—

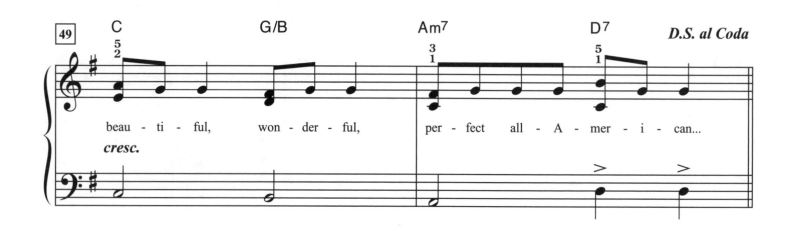

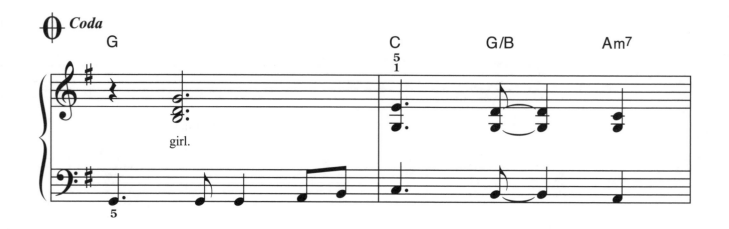

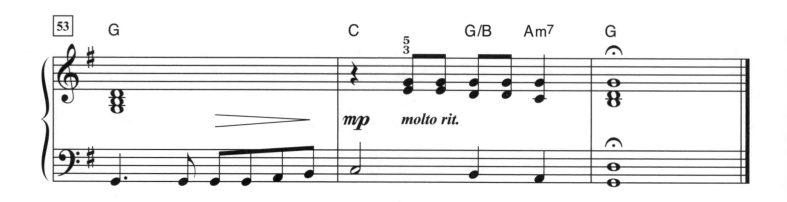

BLOWN AWAY

Words and Music by
Josh Kear and Chris Tompkins
Arranged by Dan Coates

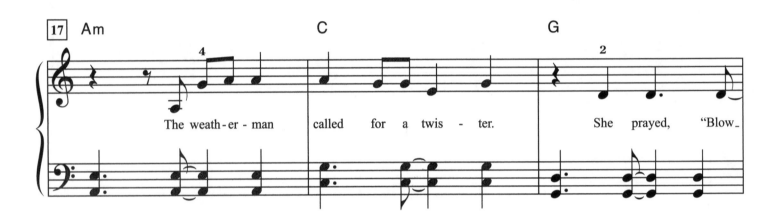

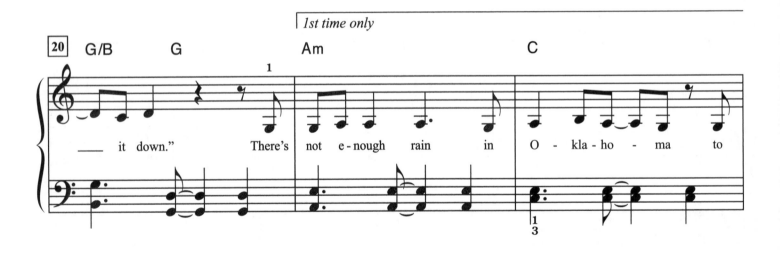

13

Chorus:

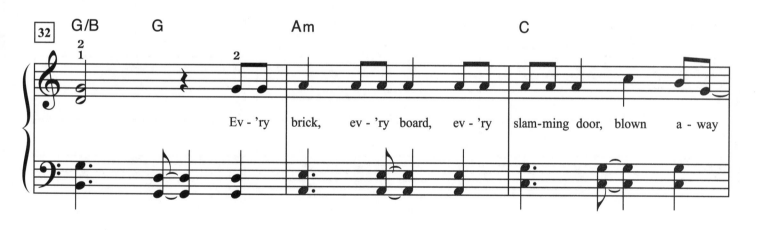

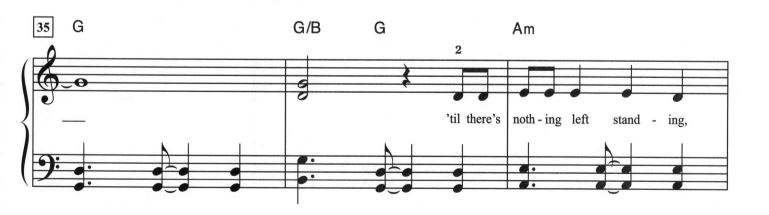

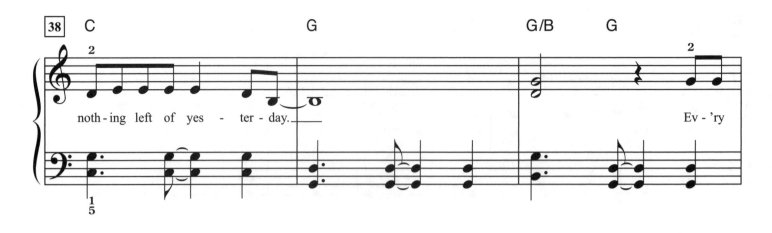

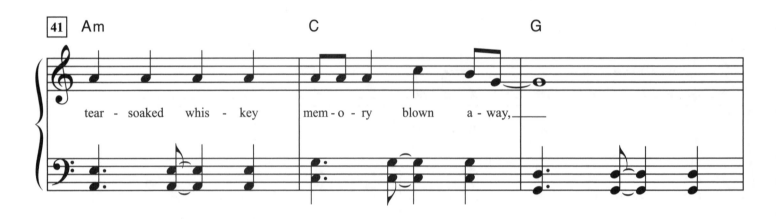

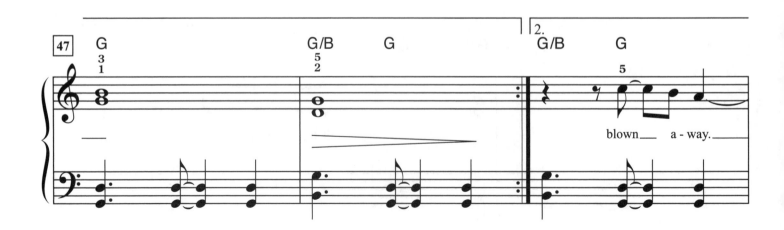

Verse 2:
She heard those sirens screaming out.
Her daddy laid there passed out on the couch.
She locked herself in the cellar,
Listened to the screaming of the wind.
Some people call it taking shelter;
She called it sweet revenge.
(To Chorus:)

DON'T IT MAKE MY BROWN EYES BLUE

Words and Music by Richard Leigh
Arranged by Dan Coates

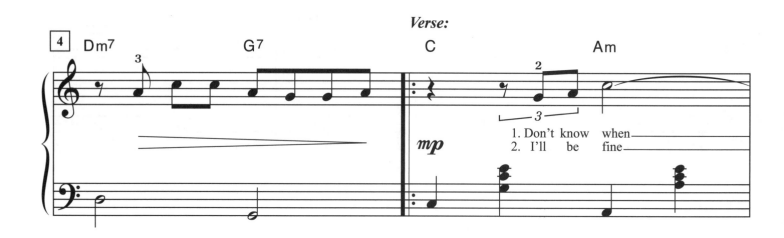

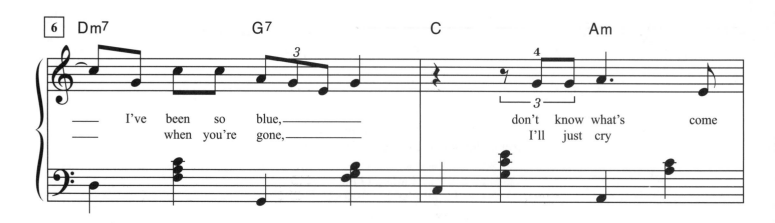

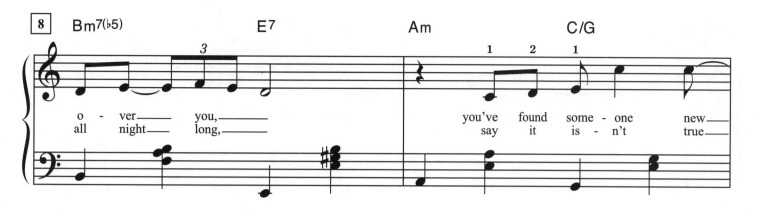

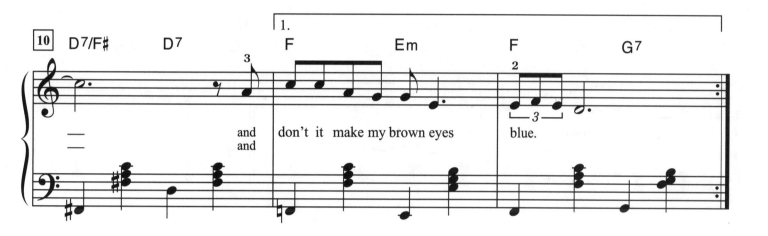

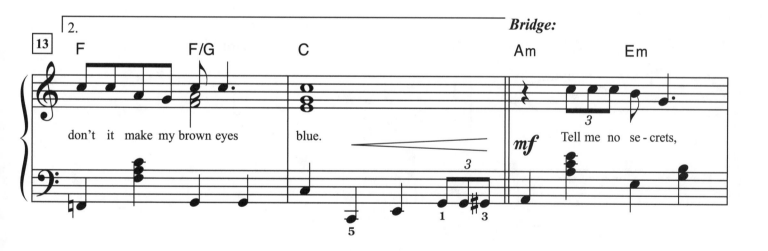

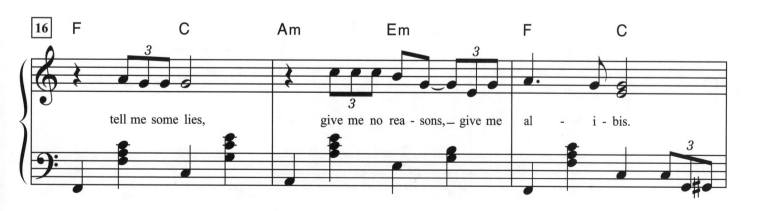

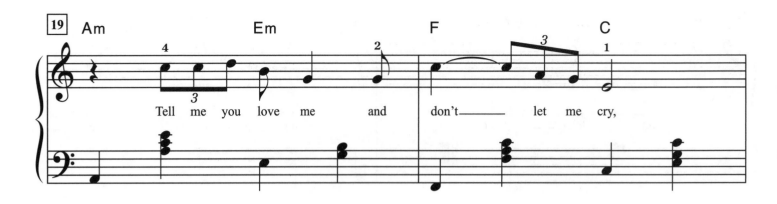

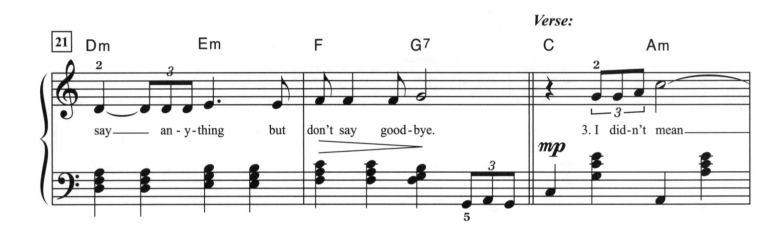

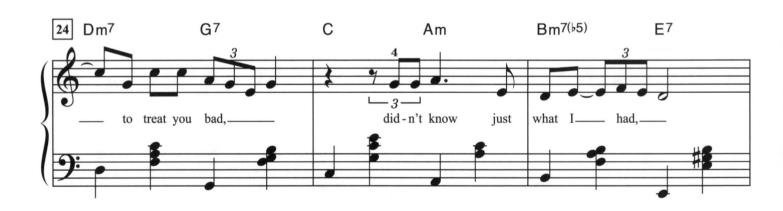

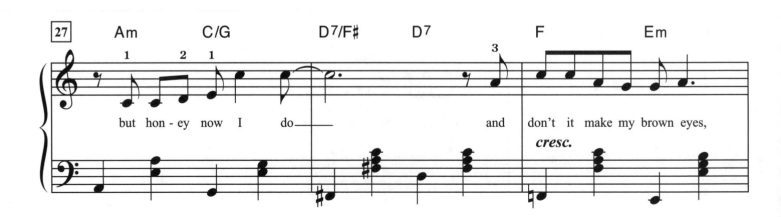

don't it make my brown eyes, don't it make my brown eyes blue.

mf

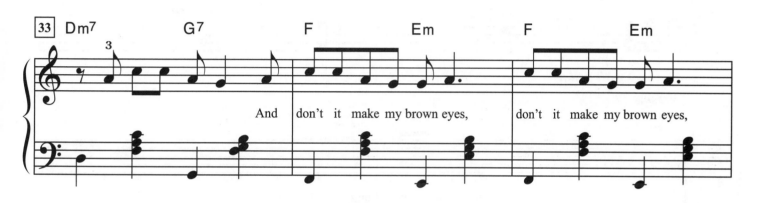

And don't it make my brown eyes, don't it make my brown eyes,

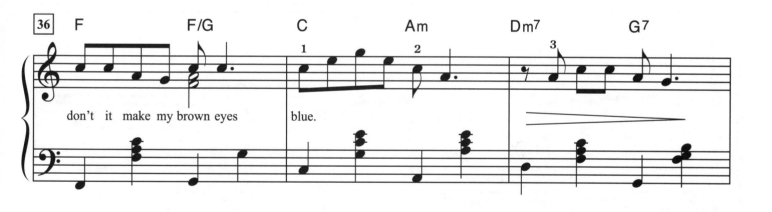

don't it make my brown eyes blue.

rit. e dim.

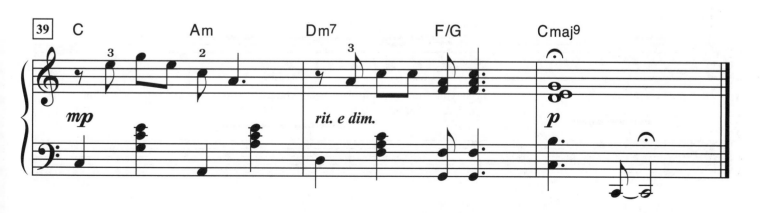

mp *p*

HOW DO I LIVE

Words and Music by Diane Warren
Arranged by Dan Coates

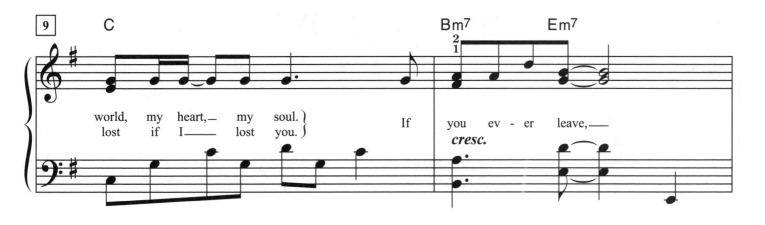

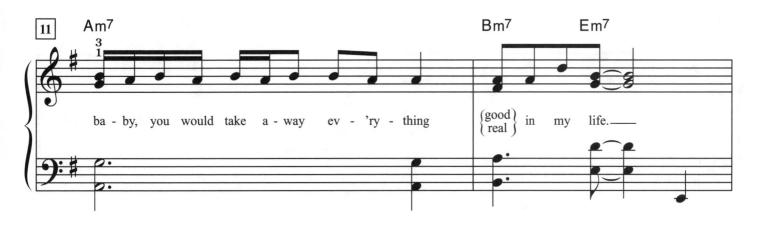

Chorus:

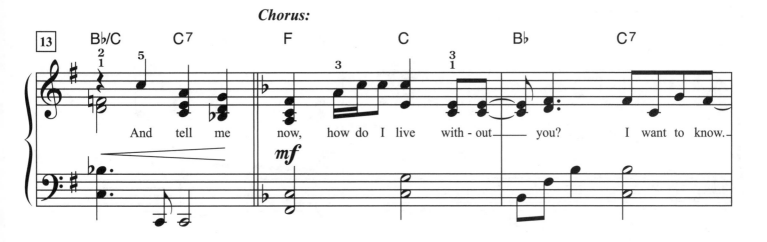

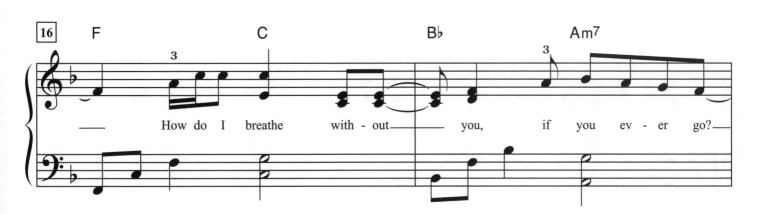

22

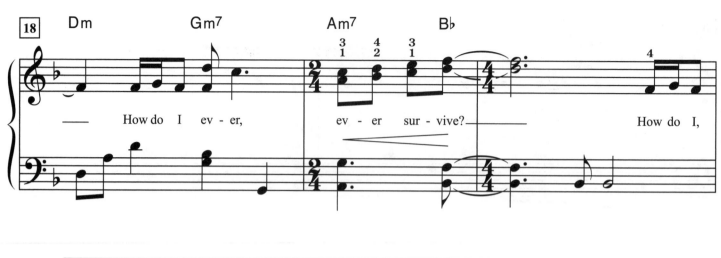

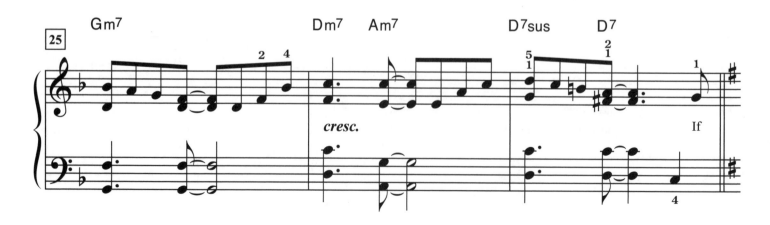

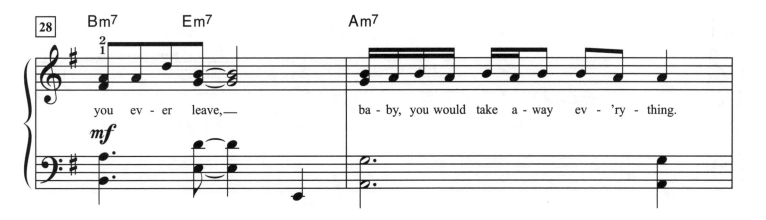

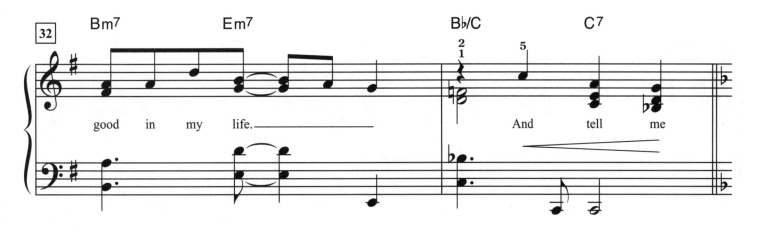

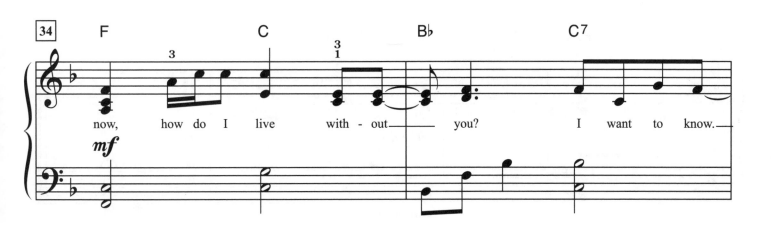

24

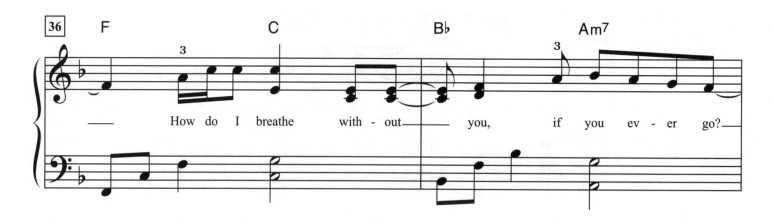

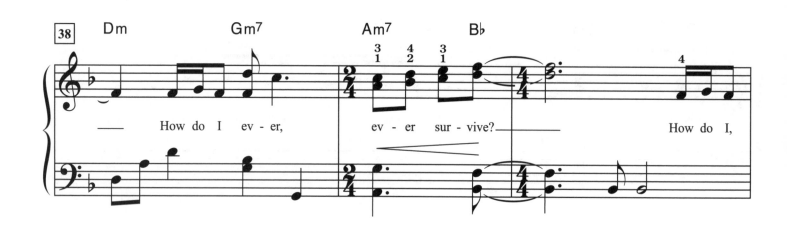

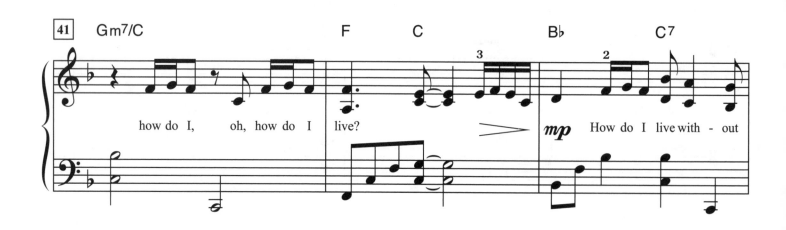

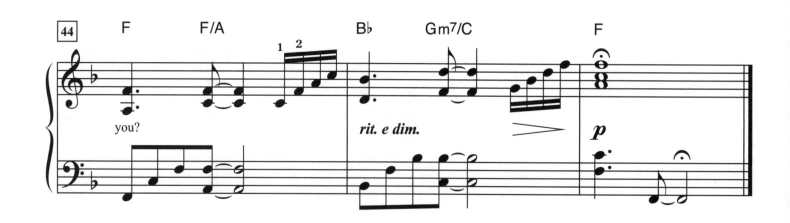

IF I DIE YOUNG

Words and Music by Kimberly Perry
Arranged by Dan Coates

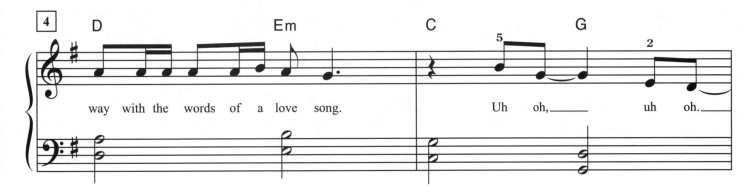

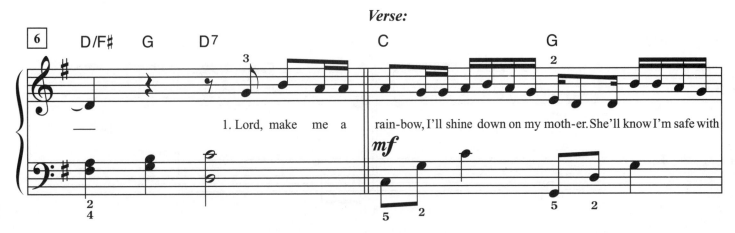

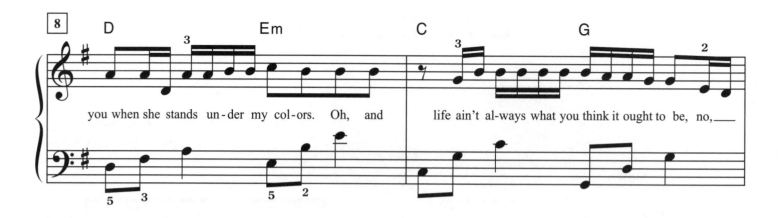

Chorus:

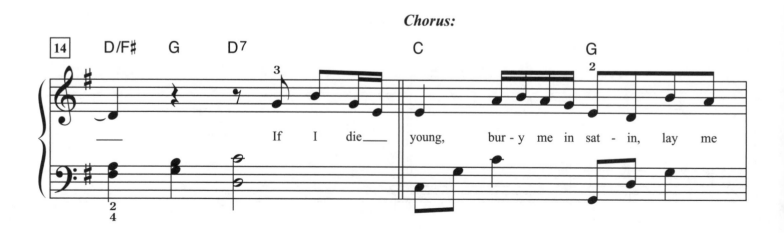

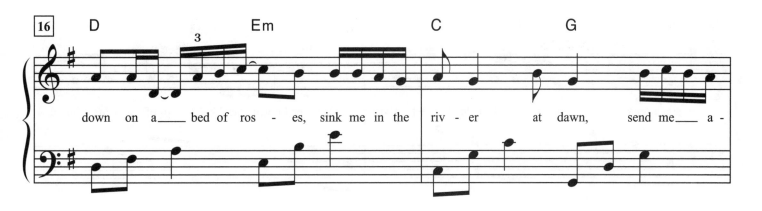

down on a___ bed of ros - es, sink me in the riv - er at dawn, send me__ a-

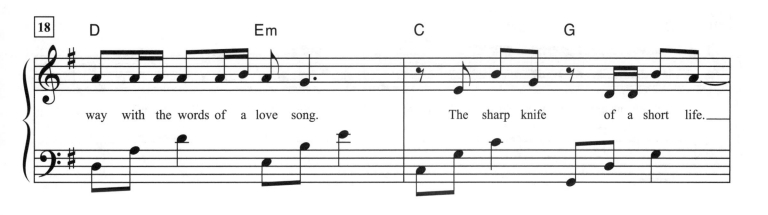

way with the words of a love song. The sharp knife of a short life.__

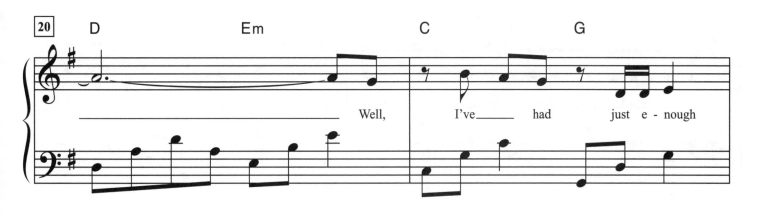

_____ Well, I've____ had just e - nough

Verse:

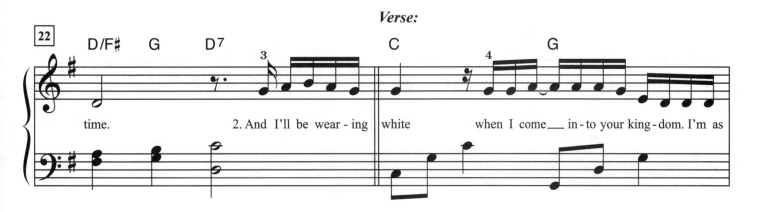

time. 2. And I'll be wear - ing white when I come__ in - to your king - dom. I'm as

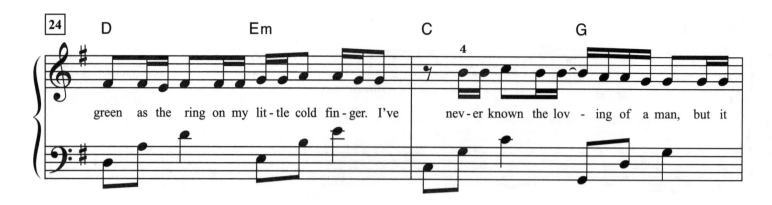

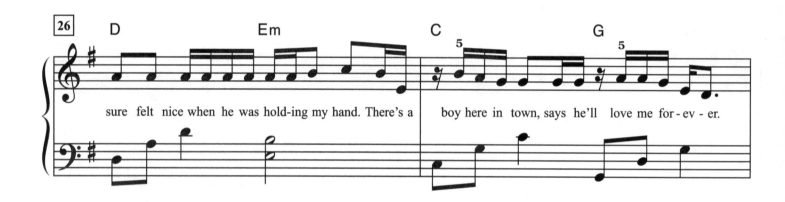

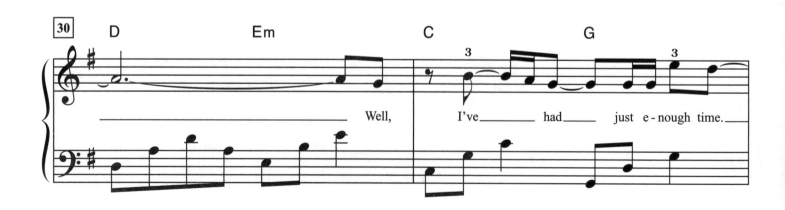

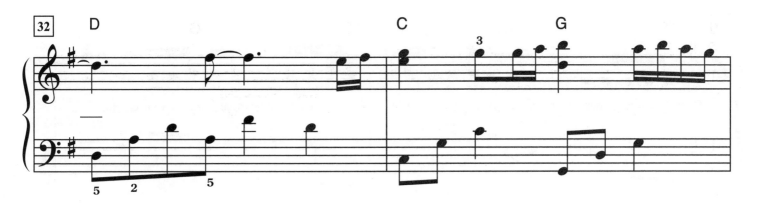

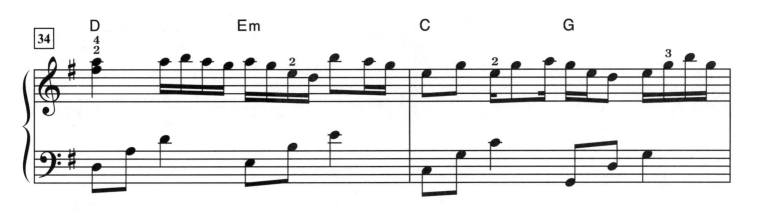

Bridge:

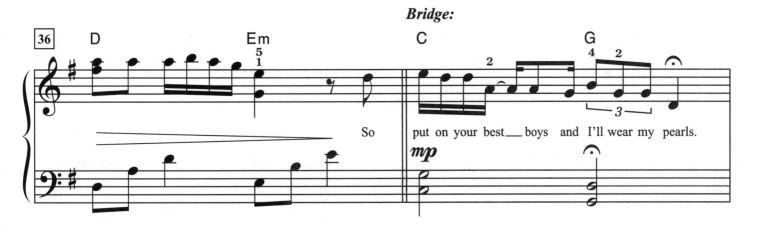

So put on your best__ boys and I'll wear my pearls.

Verse:

What I nev-er did is done. 3. A pen-ny for my thoughts, oh no, I'll sell__them for a dol-lar.

MAMA'S BROKEN HEART

Words and Music by Kacey Musgraves,
Shane McAnally and Brandy Clark
Arranged by Dan Coates

Moderately fast

Verse:

1. I cut my bangs with some rust-y kitch-en scis-sors.
2. See additional lyrics.

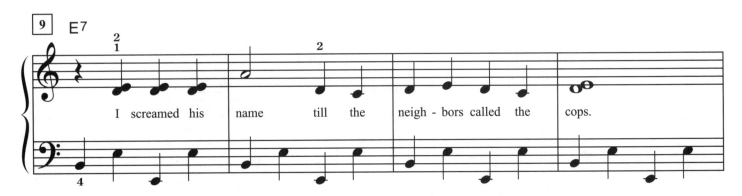

I screamed his name till the neigh-bors called the cops.

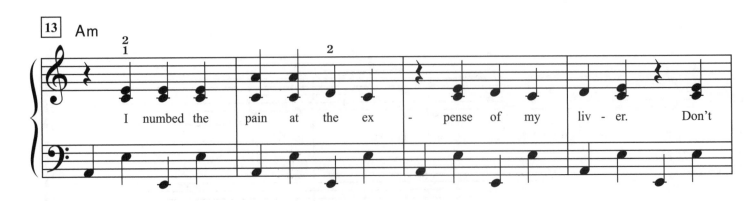

I numbed the pain at the ex - pense of my liv - er. Don't

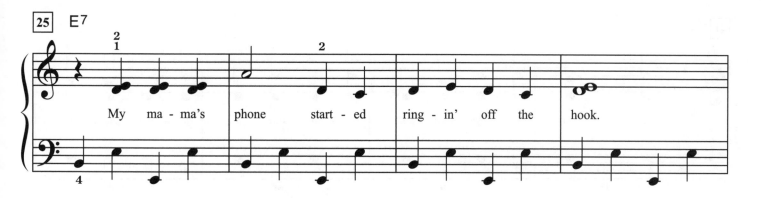

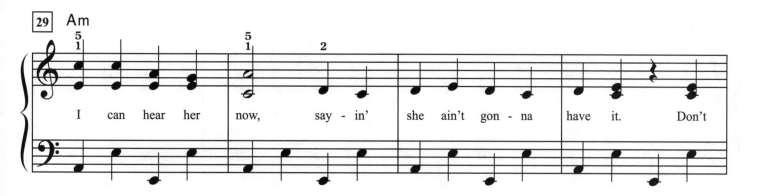

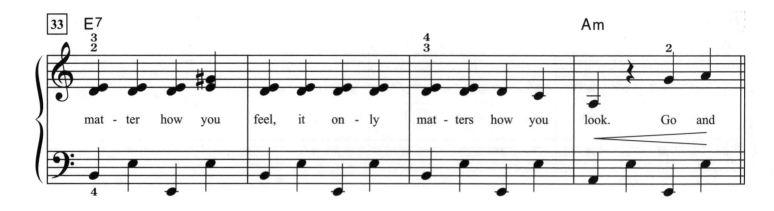

33 E7 Am

matter how you feel, it on-ly matters how you look. Go and

37 *Chorus:*

f fix your make-up, girl. It's just a break-up. Run and

41 E7

hide your cra-zy and start act-in' like a la-dy 'cause I

45 Am

raised you bet-ter. Got-ta keep it to-geth-er e-ven

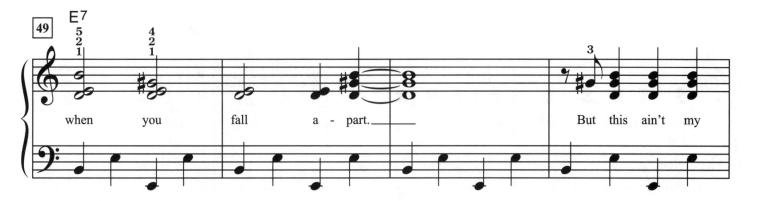

when you   fall   a - part._____   But this ain't my

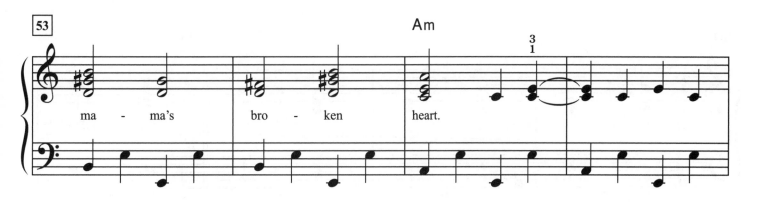

ma - ma's   bro - ken   heart.

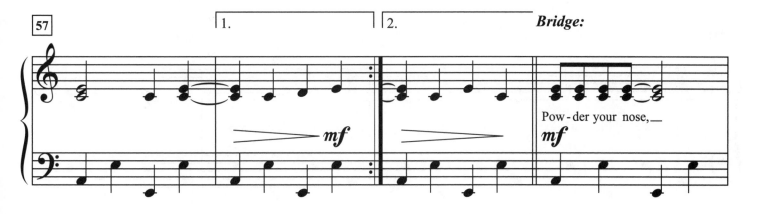

Bridge:

Pow - der your nose,___

paint your toes,___   line your lips___ and   keep 'em closed.   Cross your legs,___

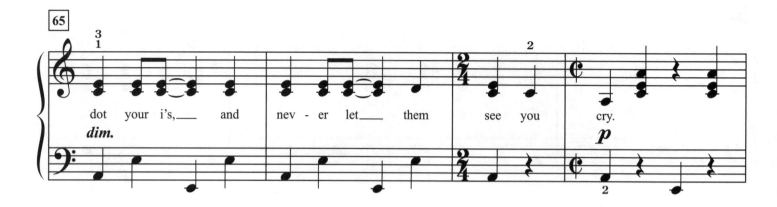

dot your i's,___ and nev - er let___ them see you cry.

dim. *p*

Chorus:

Go and fix your

f

E7

make - up, girl. It's just a break - up. Run and hide your

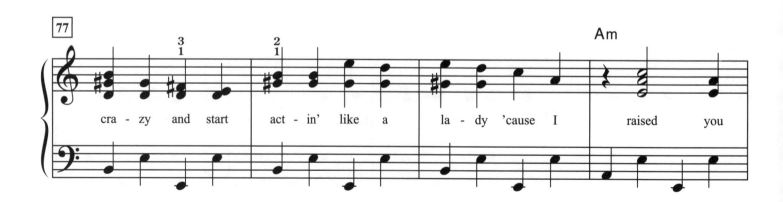

Am

cra - zy and start act - in' like a la - dy 'cause I raised you

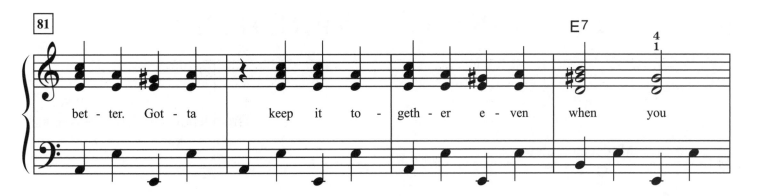

Verse 2:
I wish I could be just a little less dramatic,
Like a Kennedy when Camelot went down in flames.
Leave it to me to be holdin' the matches
When the firetrucks show up and there's nobody else to blame.
Can't get revenge and keep a spotless reputation.
Sometimes revenge is a choice you gotta make.
My mama came from a softer generation
Where you get a grip and bite your lip just to save a little face.
(To Chorus:)

LIVE LIKE YOU WERE DYING

Words and Music by
Tim Nichols and Craig Wiseman
Arranged by Dan Coates

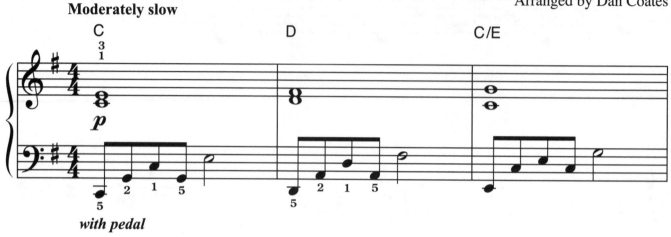

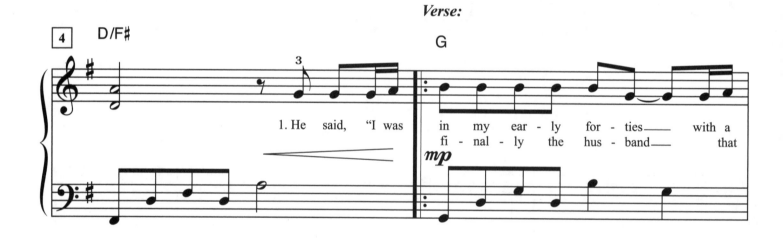

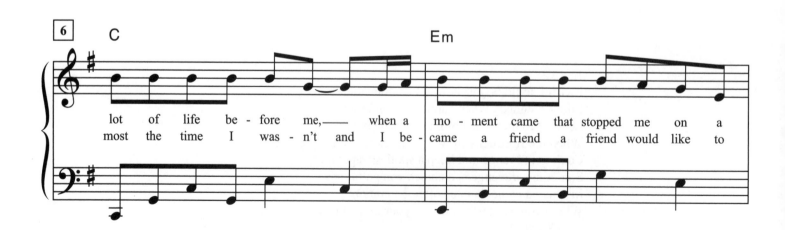

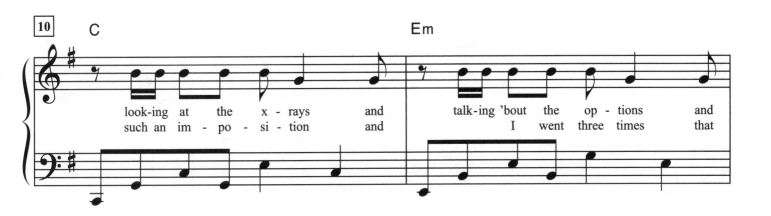

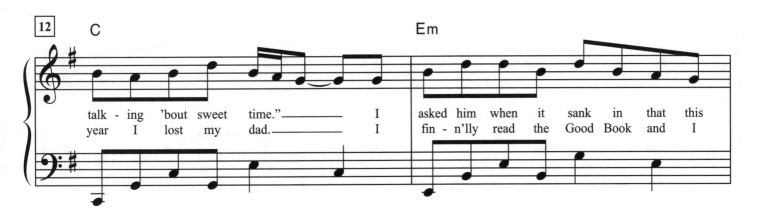

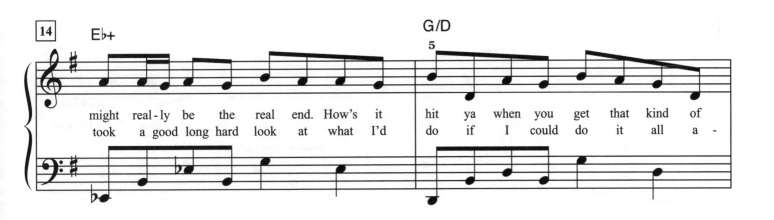

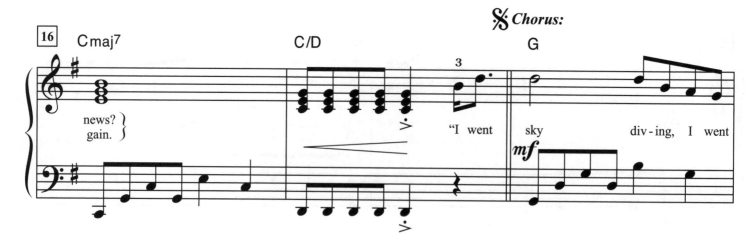

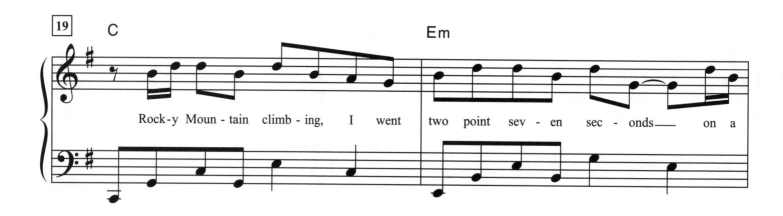

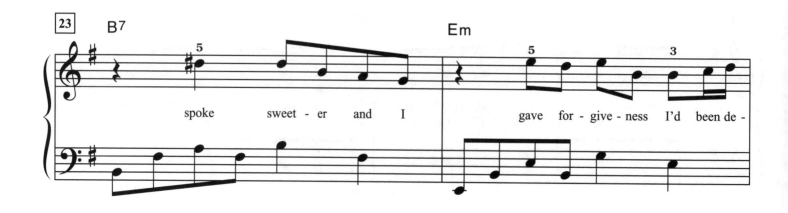

ny - ing." And he said, "Some - day I hope you get the

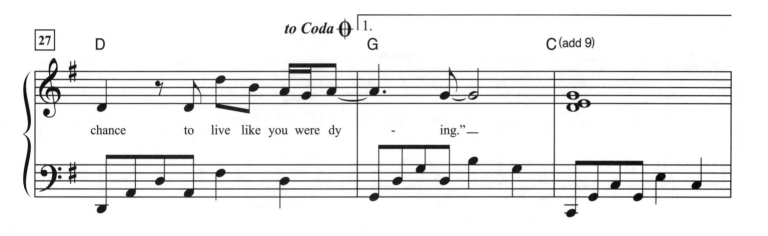

to Coda ⊕ |1.

chance to live like you were dy - ing." —

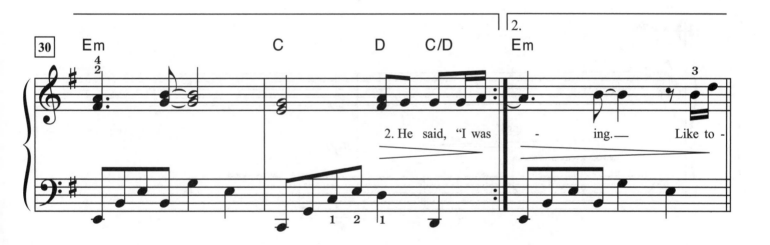

2. He said, "I was - ing. — Like to -

Bridge:

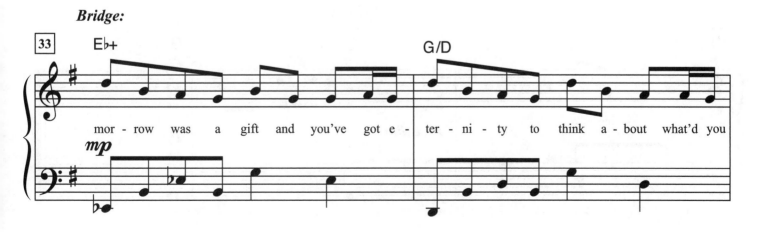

mor - row was a gift and you've got e - ter - ni - ty to think a - bout what'd you

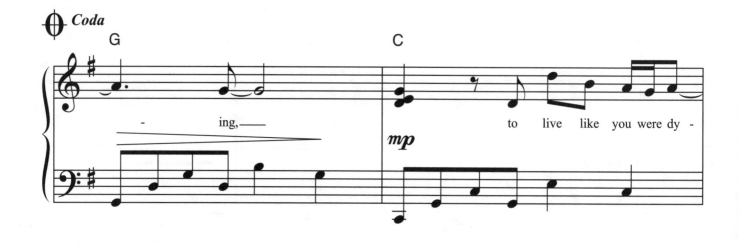

STAND BY YOUR MAN

Words and Music by
Tammy Wynette and Billy Sherrill
Arranged by Dan Coates

Moderately, with a steady beat

NEED YOU NOW

Words and Music by Dave Haywood,
Charles Kelley, Hillary Scott and Josh Kear
Arranged by Dan Coates

47

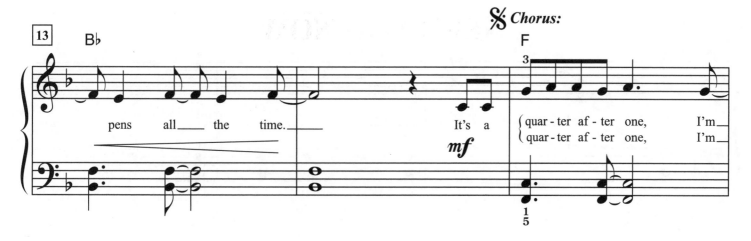

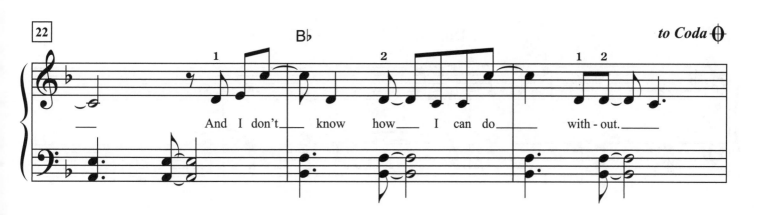

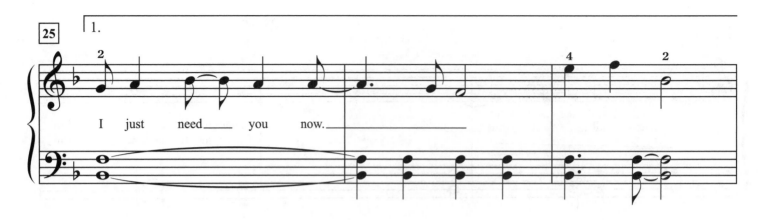

25 |1.

I just need you now.

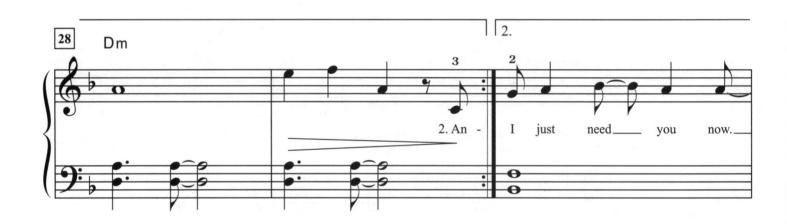

28 Dm

|2.

2. An - I just need you now.

31 Dm   C/E   F   B♭maj7

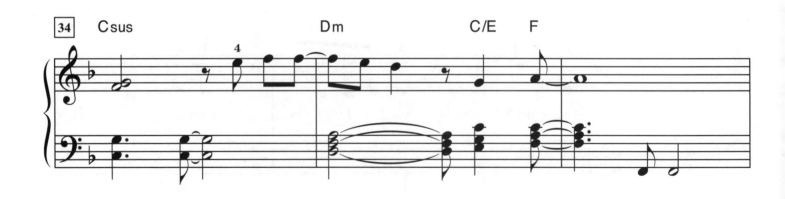

34 Csus   Dm   C/E   F

Verse 2:
Another shot of whiskey, can't stop looking at the door,
Wishing you'd come sweeping in the way you did before.
And I wonder if I ever cross your mind.
For me it happens all the time.
(To Chorus:)

TEARDROPS ON MY GUITAR

Words and Music by
Taylor Swift and Liz Rose
Arranged by Dan Coates

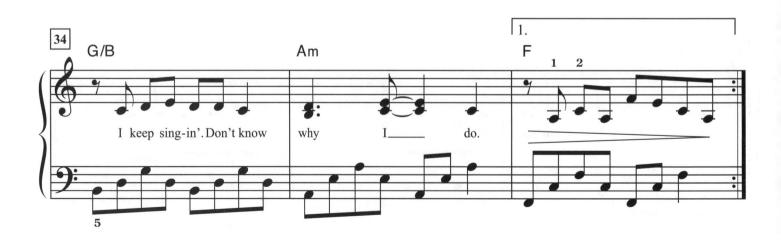

Verse 3:
Drew walks by me.
Can't he tell that I can't breathe?
And there he goes so perfectly,
The kind of flawless I wish I could be.
She better hold him tight,
Give him all her love,
Look in those beautiful eyes
And know she's lucky 'cause...
(To Chorus:)

WAGON WHEEL

Words and Music by
Ketch Secor and Bob Dylan
Arranged by Dan Coates

hop-in' for Ra - leigh. I can see my ba - by to - night._____ So

Chorus:

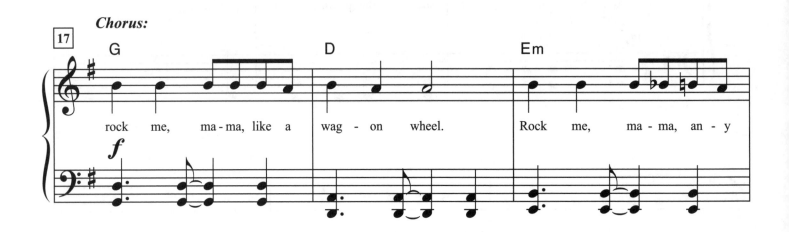

rock me, ma - ma, like a wag - on wheel. Rock me, ma - ma, an - y

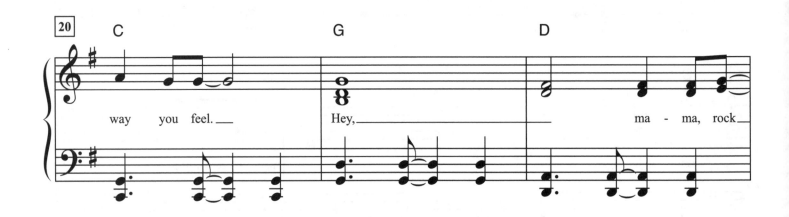

way you feel.___ Hey,_____ ma - ma, rock

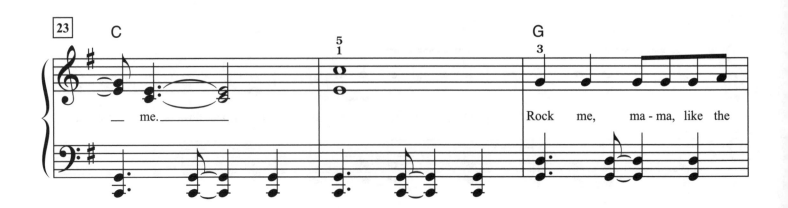

me._____ Rock me, ma - ma, like the

58

Verse 2:
Runnin' from the cold up in New England,
I was born to be a fiddler in an old-time string band.
My baby plays the guitar, I pick a banjo now.
Oh, north country winters keep a-gettin' me down.
Lost my money playin' poker, so I had to leave town.
But I ain't a-turnin' back to livin' that old life no more.
(To Chorus:)

THERE YOU'LL BE

Words and Music by Diane Warren
Arranged by Dan Coates

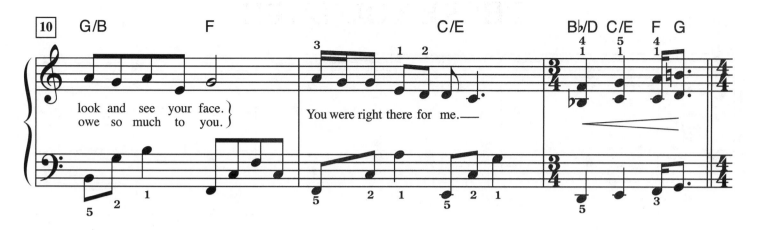

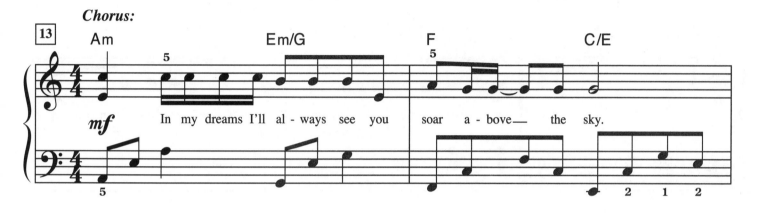

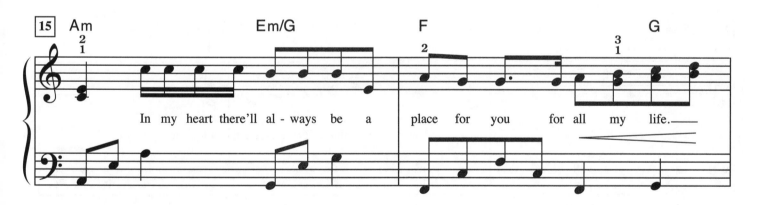

62

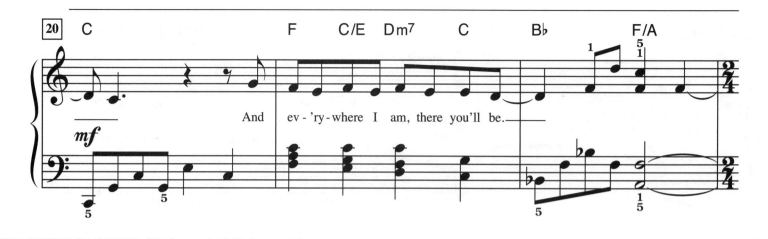

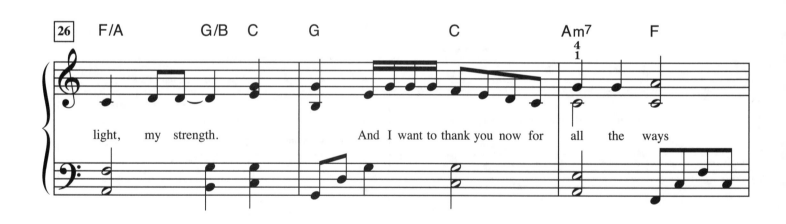

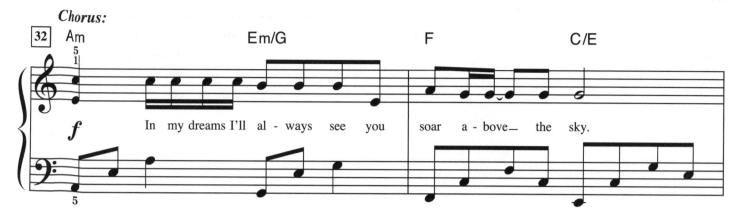

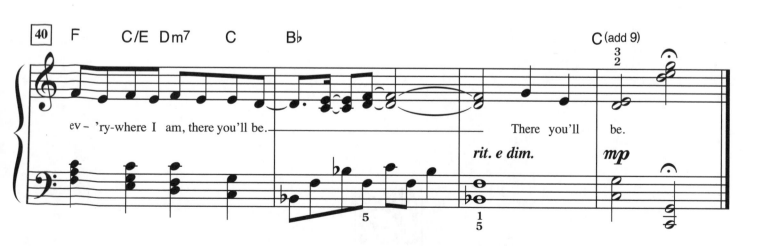